The **REAL** Story:
DEBUNKING HISTORY

THE REAL STORY BEHIND

U.S. TREATIES WITH NATIVE AMERICANS

SARAH MACHAJEWSKI

PowerKiDS press

New York

Published in 2020 by The Rosen Publishing Group, Inc.
29 East 21st Street, New York, NY 10010

First Edition

Editor: Jill Keppeler
Book Design: Reann Nye

Photo Credits: Cover Photo 12/Universal Images Group/Getty Images; p. 5 Historical Picture Archive/ Corbis Historical/Getty Images; p. 7 https://commons.wikimedia.org/wiki/File:The_First_Thanksgiving_ cph.3g04961.jpg; pp. 9, 15 bauhaus1000/DigitalVision Vectors/Getty Images; p. 10 Joseph D. Lavenburg/National Geographic/Getty Images; pp. 11, 23 Rainer Lesniewski/Shutterstock.com; p. 13 Kean Collection/ Archive Photos/Getty Images; p. 17 Album/Alamy Photos; p. 19 National Archives Catalog; p. 21 Underwood Archives/Archive Photos/Getty Images; p. 25 https://commons.wikimedia. org/wiki/File:Chiricahua_Apaches_Four_Months_After_Arriving_at_Carlisle.jpg; p. 27 Pictorial Parade/ Archive Photos/Getty Images; p. 28 Pacific Press/LightRocket/Getty Images; p. 29 Bloomberg/Getty Images.

Cataloging-in-Publication Data

Names: Machajewski, Sarah.
Title: The real story behind U.S. treaties with Native Americans / Sarah Machajewski.
Description: New York : PowerKids Press, 2020. | Series: The real story: debunking history | Includes glossary and index.
Identifiers: ISBN 9781538344705 (pbk.) | ISBN 9781538343470 (library bound) | ISBN 9781538344712 (6 pack)
Subjects: LCSH: Indians of North America–Treaties–Juvenile literature. | Indians of North America–Government relations–Juvenile literature.
Classification: LCC E95.M33 2020 | DDC 346.7301'3–dc23

Manufactured in the United States of America

CPSIA Compliance Information: Batch #CSPK19. For Further Information contact Rosen Publishing, New York, New York at 1-800-237-9932

CONTENTS

IN PURSUIT OF TRUTH

Long ago, before the United States became a country and before Europeans arrived in North America, ancestors of today's Native Americans lived across the continent, from the Pacific Northwest to the southeastern tip of Florida. As the original people to call North America home, Native Americans saw their lives changed forever when white settlers arrived and claimed the land for themselves.

Many of these changes were later **documented** in treaties that were signed by the United States government and native tribes. Treaties addressed the rights and citizenship of native people, determined land boundaries, and claimed to provide certain protections. But were these treaties honored as intended, or did they become broken promises? By the end of this book, you'll be asked to decide for yourself.

USING PREFERRED TERMS

According to the Bureau of Indian Affairs, "American Indian" and "Alaska Native" are the preferred terms for people who belong to a federally recognized tribe in the United States. "Native American" is used to describe "all Native peoples of the United States and its territories, including American Indians, Alaska Natives, Native Hawaiians, Chamorros, and American Samoans, as well as persons from Canada First Nations and . . . communities in Mexico and Central and South America who are U.S. residents." However, each person decides which term is right for them.

4

What is the real truth behind U.S. treaties with Native Americans? Only by studying history with a critical eye can we hope to find out.

UNDERSTANDING THE HISTORY

Because their ancestors were the first to come to and live in North America, Native Americans are considered the original people of the continent. Throughout history, this status has shaped the questions of land ownership, territories, borders, and rights that Native Americans are entitled to, and how white society has responded.

When Europeans arrived in the Americas, they expected to find a whole continent for the taking. However, they found it occupied by many tribes that had organized societies, strong traditions, and established leaders. From these early colonial days, tribal nations were considered sovereign, or independent. Their interactions with the U.S. government have been guided by this status. For a period of about 100 years, these interactions often involved treaty making.

A LAND OF MANY

It's often said that the United States is a land of immigrants because the racial and **ethnic** groups represented in America have roots elsewhere. Most Americans have family who arrived in America from faraway places. Native Americans, however, can trace their ancestry on this continent back thousands of years before most ethnic groups, before ships carried non-native people to their homelands. Researchers believe the first peoples came to the Americas across a land bridge from Asia.

Many untruths are told about native **culture** and society because much of history was recorded and told by white newcomers. It's important to consult many sources and listen to many voices in order to find the truth.

SUPREME LAW

Treaties are legal agreements that are part of what the U.S. Constitution refers to as "the supreme law of the land." Treaties signed between native tribes and the United States are viewed the same as treaties with foreign nations.

Native American treaties are supposed to have a lot of power because they were made under the U.S. Constitution. It's important to note that these treaties don't give rights to native peoples. They acknowledge the rights that native peoples have always had as America's original peoples. Native people were told that the treaties they signed would protect them, but this wasn't true. The real story of Native American treaties is that the United States has **violated** most, if not all, of them.

UPHELD OR NOT?

You may think that anyone who signs a treaty would follow it, but this isn't always the case. One way to see if treaties have been followed is to read the language of the treaty and then compare it to a trusted, factual source that describes what actually happened. These may include encyclopedias, well-known institutions, and nonprofit or ".org" websites. Sources written with a strong opinion can't always be trusted.

FACT FINDER

Native American nations and the U.S. government signed about 370 treaties from 1778 to 1871. This process is no longer in practice today.

Many see the United States' failure to pay tribal nations for their land and to provide the support they were promised as the cause of many social and economic problems facing Native Americans today.

TREATY OF CANANDAIGUA, 1794

The Treaty of Canandaigua was an early treaty between native nations and the U.S. government. About 1,600 representatives of the Haudenosaunee Confederacy, also called the Six Nations, met with U.S. government officials to sign the treaty on November 11, 1794, a little more than 10 years after the end of the Revolutionary War and the founding of the United States.

This treaty established peace between the Haudenosaunee peoples and the United States, recognized the Six Nations as sovereign, and called for the United States to return more than a million acres of land to the Haudenosaunee. However, since that time, the U.S. people and government have made many attempts to build on or cross into the Haudenosaunee lands that the treaty is supposed to protect.

FACT FINDER

The Seneca, Mohawk, Onondaga, Cayuga, Oneida, and Tuscarora peoples belong to the Six Nations.

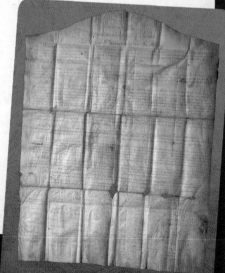

AN ORIGINAL COPY OF THE CANANDAIGUA TREATY OF 1794

The Treaty of Canandaigua stated that the U.S. would provide $4,500 in goods to the Haudenosaunee annually. This specific term is still honored today, as is, for the most part, the agreement of peace and friendship between nations.

SIX NATIONS TERRITORY

SENECA

TUSCARORA

CAYUGA

ONEIDA

ONONDAGA

MOHAWK

TREATY OF FORT WAYNE, 1809

As more settlers came to the United States, land became a large concern. Native nations had a lot of land, and the growing United States wanted it. Many treaties deal with the question of land ownership, including the Treaty of Fort Wayne.

Signed in 1809, the treaty took about 3 million acres (1.2 million ha) of Indian land and gave it to the United States for about 2 cents per acre—far below fair asking price. Many tribal leaders hesitated to sign it at first, but they gave in under growing pressure from the U.S. government. Two years later, William Henry Harrison, an official who signed the treaty and later became president, led an attack on the native people. Decades later, they were forcibly removed from their land.

AN UNPOPULAR DECISION

Some native peoples disagreed with the Treaty of Fort Wayne. Some tribal members questioned how much whites were occupying their land, while the Shawnee chief Tecumseh questioned whether the tribal leaders could sell off land that was shared by many nations. When the United States later violated the treaty terms, war broke out.

Tecumseh and his followers later fought Harrison's troops in 1813, at the Battle of the Thames in Ontario, Canada. Tecumseh died in the battle, which was part of the War of 1812.

13

MANIFEST DESTINY

In the 1800s, after the end of the War of 1812, the country entered an era of westward expansion. Thousands of people moved west of the Mississippi River and settled on land that, until then, only native people had occupied. Much of this land was rich with valuable metals and minerals, building materials, and other resources that would help grow the United States' economy and its riches.

Westward expansion was, in part, a result of the idea of "manifest destiny," which said Americans should go west, tame the wild frontier, and stretch across the continent. This idea was used to support the purchase (or theft) of much land. One side of the story is that this helped the United States become a rich and powerful country. But what does the other side say?

FACT FINDER

The era of "manifest destiny" began around 1803 with the Louisiana Purchase and ended around 1848 with the end of the U.S.-Mexican War.

Some stories about westward expansion praise white
settlers for seeking new opportunities in the West. But
other sources tell of how this caused many problems and
much suffering for Native Americans. In history, the same
event can have many perspectives, or points of view.

THE INDIAN REMOVAL ACT

The treatment of southeastern Indian tribes during this time reveals a clear look at the problems many native peoples faced. In 1814, Andrew Jackson defeated the Creek Indians in the Southeast and forced upon them a treaty that saw the surrender of 20 million acres (8.1 million ha) of their land to the U.S. government. Over the next 10 years, the United States arranged 11 treaties that forced native peoples off their land and onto **reservations**.

This reached a peak with the Indian Removal Act of 1830. This act, passed when Jackson was president, granted land in the West to the Cherokee, Creek, Chickasaw, Choctaw, and Seminole peoples— but also forced them to move there, generally under horrible conditions. This, especially the **ordeal** of the Cherokee, was called the Trail of Tears.

FACT FINDER

About 100,000 Native Americans were forced to move during the Trail of Tears, and about 15,000 died on the journey.

AGREEING TO APPEASE

As white settlers poured into the Southeast, they asked the U.S. government to get rid of the Native Americans they felt were living on "their" land. While some tribes fought back against this, as time went on, some felt they could do nothing to stop the larger, more powerful United States. They tried to **appease** the United States instead, hoping that they could keep some land by giving up much of it. It didn't work—the United States took everything.

Gather facts about westward expansion and the Trail of Tears.
Compare the native perspective of this time to the white
perspective of this time. What conclusions can you draw?

TREATY OF MEDICINE CREEK, 1854

Perspectives can change over time, and people can view history through a new lens. Today, historians agree the United States violated nearly every Indian treaty it signed. Such is the case of the Treaty of Medicine Creek, which was signed in 1854.

The Nisqually, Puyallup, Squaxin Island, and other Pacific Northwestern groups signed this treaty with the United States. The Native American groups surrendered 2.5 million acres (1 million ha) of land for money and certain conditions. Not long later, this treaty was viewed with regret. But in the 1960s and 1970s, native peoples called on the wording of this treaty as they stood up for their rights surrounding hunting and fishing territories. Today, many tribal members view parts of this treaty as a step toward strengthening native rights and sovereignty.

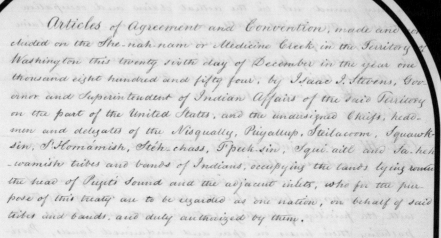

Articles of *Agreement* and *Convention*, made and concluded on the She-nah-nam or Medicine Creek in the Territory of Washington this twenty sixth day of December in the year one thousand eight hundred and fifty four, by Isaac I. Stevens, Governor and Superintendent of Indian Affairs of the said Territory on the part of the United States, and the undersigned Chiefs, headmen and delegates of the Nisqually, Puyallup, Steilacoom, Squawksin, S'Homamish, Steh-chass, T'peeh-sin, Squi-aitl and Sa-heh-wamish tribes and bands of Indians, occupying the lands lying round the head of Puget Sound and the adjacent inlets, who for the purpose of this treaty are to be regarded as one nation, on behalf of said tribes and bands, and duly authorized by them.

Art. I   The said tribes and bands of Indians hereby cede, relinquish and convey to the United States all their right, title and interest in and to the lands and country occupied by them, bounded and described as follows, to wit:

Commencing at the point on the eastern side of Admiralty Inlet, known as Point Pully, about midway between Commencement and Elliott Bays; thence running in a South easterly direction, following the divide between the waters of the Puyallup and Dwamish or White rivers to the summit of the Cascade Mountains, thence Southerly along the summit of said range to a point opposite the main source of the Skookum Chuck Creek, thence and down said Creek to the coal mine, thence Northwesterly to the summit of the Black Hills, thence northerly to the upper forks of the Sat-sop river, thence Northeasterly through the portage known as Wilkes' portage to Point Southworth on the western side of Admiralty Inlet, thence around the foot of Vashon's Island South easterly to the place of beginning.

The Treaty of Medicine Creek was one of four treaties made between the United States and Pacific Northwestern tribes during this time.

UNRATIFIED TREATIES IN CALIFORNIA

During the California gold rush of the mid-1800s, thousands of fortune seekers flooded into California territory, which had great consequences for the native peoples in the area. The U.S. Army, still in the area because of the U.S.-Mexican War, restricted where Native Americans could go, banned them from testifying, or speaking, in court, and denied their right to vote.

Just a few years later, California's native peoples signed 18 treaties with the United States to sell their land and receive reservations in return. However, the U.S. Senate never ratified, or approved, these treaties. In fact, the Senate was ordered to keep the unratified treaties a secret, a cover-up that caused native people to suffer in silence without the reservation land or the money they were promised.

FACT FINDER

In 1905, the U.S. government looked into the events surrounding the unratified treaties. The investigation concluded "that no **compensation** has ever been made the California Indians for their lands, as the Government seems to have... [not recognized] the Indians' right of occupancy."

After reading about the unratified treaties of California, consider the following questions. Why do you think the government attempted to keep the treaties a secret? What were the consequences, and what does it say about the country's treatment of Indian nations?

THE ISSUE OF THE BLACK HILLS

The Fort Laramie Treaty, signed in 1868, established peace between the Sioux Nation and the United States and provided reservation land within the Black Hills of South Dakota.

The treaty said the Sioux had the only rights to the Black Hills, which are their sacred territory. But after gold was discovered there, gold seekers ignored the treaty entirely. In 1874, the U.S. Army invaded Sioux territory and launched an attack on the bands of Indians who were rightfully there. In 1877, the United States took the land, despite the treaty. Of this time, Spotted Tail, a Sioux man, remarked, "This war was brought upon us by [people] who came to take our land from us without price." Today, the Sioux are still fighting to get their land back.

LEARNING FROM PRIMARY SOURCES

It's important to listen to people's voices, especially if they're from a group or culture that has been silenced. Primary sources provide a better look into history with a firsthand or eyewitness account. Primary sources include journal entries, newspaper articles, photographs, and paintings. Legal documents, scientific papers, video footage, and speeches are primary sources, too. They provide an opportunity to learn what people who experienced history thought or felt, bringing us closer to the truth.

FACT FINDER

The U.S. government has ruled that the Sioux are owed what's now more than $1.3 billion in compensation for the land that was taken from them. The Sioux refuse to accept the money, as they feel their land should be returned instead.

The map below shows the land promised to the Sioux in 1868 and the amount of land they have today. After comparing the maps, do you think the United States honored what it promised in the Fort Laramie Treaty? Why or why not?

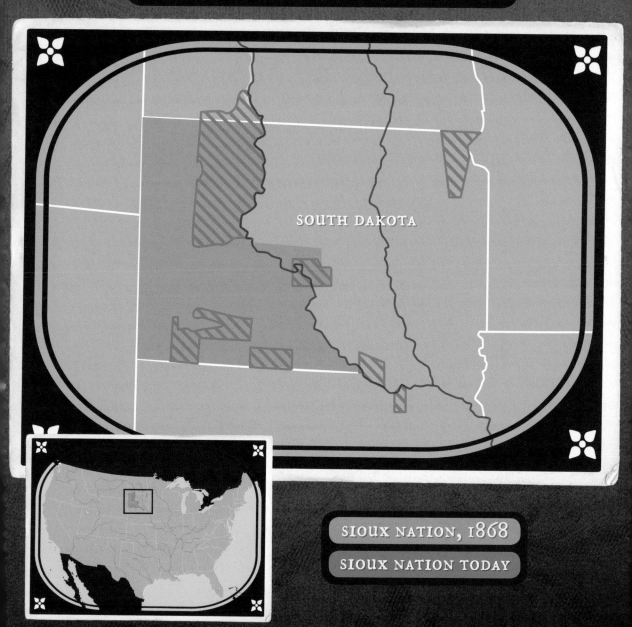

SOUTH DAKOTA

SIOUX NATION, 1868

SIOUX NATION TODAY

THE END OF TREATY MAKING

The United States government stopped making treaties with Native American nations in 1871. This practice came to an end with the passing of the Indian Appropriations Act. According to this act, the federal government no longer recognized native groups as independent nations.

The United States' refusal to acknowledge native groups as nations was a sign of discrimination, or unfair treatment. As one congressman observed at the time, many people believed "they are simply not independent nations whom we are to treat as our equals." This was reflected in the way Native Americans were treated in the years to come. Children were sent to boarding schools where they were forced to **assimilate**. Native people were denied U.S. citizenship until 1924.

THE REASONS WHY

The shift in Indian policy reflected the growing belief that tribal nations were no longer strong or powerful. The truth is that they were often weakened by more than a century of war and disease, as well as poor conditions on reservations, where people often lacked proper food, health care and housing. If native nations were to be punished for no longer being strong, the punishment ignored the factors that led them there.

FACT FINDER

Indian boarding schools forced native children to assimilate into white society by cutting their hair, making them speak English, and making them ignore their traditions.

Historically, Native Americans were **stereotyped** as being savage or simple. Some whites felt education could make them "better." In reality, this is a **racist** idea that caused many people to suffer.

INDIAN POWER AND SELF-DETERMINATION

Federal policy toward Native Americans changed again in the 1960s and 1970s following a period of Native American **activism**. While native peoples had long stood up against **oppression**, organized resistance groups began fighting to protect land rights and to improve opportunities for native people. Some people exercised their treaty rights through "fish-ins," calling on the fishing and hunting rights protected under the Treaty of Medicine Creek.

These events were the beginning of a movement that fought for self-determination. This is the idea that tribes should govern themselves. This period was important in advancing Native American rights. Importantly, it exposed the truth about the federal government's treatment of Native Americans to a national audience.

TRAIL OF BROKEN TREATIES

In 1972, Indian activists gathered in Minneapolis and created a list of demands to present to the U.S. government. The protestors wanted the government to honor the treaties it had made with Indian nations. They traveled to Washington, D.C., and occupied the Bureau of Indian Affairs building for six days. The journey, which they called the Trail of Broken Treaties, brought much national attention to the movement.

This group of Native Americans is protesting in 1972 on the steps of the Bureau of Indian Affairs building in Washington, D.C.

REAL CONSEQUENCES

In 2016, members of the Standing Rock Sioux tribe and others organized to protest the building of an oil pipeline through their sacred, "protected" lands. The pipeline has been built, despite protests—proof that while the government no longer makes treaties, it continues to violate them.

While the false history of Indian treaties has long been debunked, the real story continues to have real consequences. The U.S. Supreme Court has heard many cases that raise questions about tribal self-governance, Indian rights, and the relationship between nations. Today, with the truth readily available, it is the responsibility of the U.S. government to weigh questions of how to honor history, respect tribal nations as sovereign, and ultimately keep its word in ways it has previously failed to do.

Protests against the Dakota Access Pipeline gathered people from many different native groups and other backgrounds to call for more protections for native sovereignty.

WITH AN INVESTIGATIVE EYE

It has taken centuries to reveal the truth behind Native American treaties. As new information comes out, it may go against what you've learned in school, from the Internet, or from other people.

When you're confronted with differing information, you can work through it if you're careful. It's important to look at different perspectives about the same topic. You should compare multiple sources to see what groups have said about a subject and why. You can question what you read, who wrote it, and what their motives are. You can analyze, or carefully study, information and form your own opinion about something. Most importantly, be open minded and willing to hear all sides of the story. It's the only way to know what truly happened.

GLOSSARY

activism: Acting strongly in support of or against an issue.

appease: To give in to another's demand to please them or make things easier.

assimilate: To absorb into the cultural tradition of a population.

compensation: Something that is done or given to make up for something else.

culture: The beliefs and ways of life of a certain group of people.

document: To record something. Or, a formal piece of writing.

ethnic: Belonging to a certain group of people who have a culture that is different from the main culture of a country.

oppression: The act of treating a person or group of people in a cruel or unfair way.

ordeal: An experience that is very unpleasant or very difficult.

racist: Following the belief that one group or race of people is better than another group or race.

reservation: Land set aside by the government for specific Native American tribes to live on.

stereotype: To believe unfairly that all people or things with a particular characteristic are the same.

violate: To fail to respect someone's rights.

INDEX

WEBSITES

Due to the changing nature of Internet links, PowerKids Press has developed an online list of websites related to the subject of this book. This site is updated regularly. Please use this link to access the list: www.powerkidslinks.com/debunk/treaties